PROLOGUE

BE PREPARED

The journey you are about to undertake is an emotional journey through the realms of the creative mind of yours truly: Shawn LaVette.

The poetry found in this collection is a reflection of the many experiences which I have been blessed enough to survive and overcome; some of which are clear (in my work) -the remainder not as conspicuous. My beginning to write became a way that I would remind myself that I had adequate training on how to overcome most hardships in the best ways. Writing down the reminder helped make it real.

I, in no way, am under the impression that I know it all. I do believe our Lord lent me the capacity to learn whatever may be required for me to pass life's tests: my duty is to follow through once the best way has been revealed to me (mentally).

When/once we wise up, we must be man/woman enough to follow through and

1

live up (Live up to fulfilling the requirements of what the best decision requires).

This collection, among other things, is a product of my intention to stay motivated, to be inspired, dream about love and lay my heart upon each and every line.

In the process: I give you something to smile about; A reminder. I lend you my own, customized personal therapy that I pray will reach you and inspire good things.

I have written you inspiration. I am taking you on a journey: You will be moved.

This collection will show you that I have something to say and I pray that my statement shall serve you well.

This is what I wrote when I could not speak.

WHEN I CAN'T SPEAK

By: Shawn LaVette

TABLE OF CONTENTS

9

Dedication

This book is dedicated to life;
Dedicated to its beauty;
To all of life's challenges;
To her ugly.
Life.
This is for you:
I love you.

UNDEFEATED

Practice can be grueling,
And the season can be tiresome;
But we have got to keep our feet moving,
We must keep our eyes up:
To adjust,
To see and do what must...
Be done;
To execute, to make it through this play,
To Win:
Today.

This day:
This opponent is one of many;
And if we keep our head in the game we will
be winning.
Overcome, learn
And execute.
And those who say you can't, well...
They'll have to lose to you too.
So get out there and win,
Make it through life's seasons.
Train, and grow, and learn if you lose;
Stay true: Be Undefeated.

EXTRA ORDINARY

You add extra to my ordinary,
And you do it in ways which help me believe;
Believe in God,
Believe in me,
And believe in what I can achieve.

You put extra with my ordinary,
And you put it there when you're with me;
By the presence that you have,
To my ordinary times you add,
And the sum is me happy when you're with
me.

You place extra in my ordinary,
And you deliver it through your
companionship,
By the company you possess,
Your being inspires my best,
And I value every aspect of our relationship.

You are a plus,
And truly add with your one of a kind;
If they are down- you're up,
And your quality helps my bland to shine.
Cause your extra is,
And your extra gives,
Motivation to each and every breath;
Cause your extra lives,
And it makes me feel,
Like I do not have any ordinary left.

HECKLER

You will win anyway,
Remain focused in the game,
Defeat your opponent –ignore the heckler.
On the sideline;
Not even in the game;
A spectator,
Observant:
More than likely a lame.
Stalking,
Watching,
Not even the real paparazzi,
Can't afford cameras,
Don't qualify as amateurs,
Holdin 'em cause they're jocking.
Speaking loud
Exciting the crowd,
Against you: they're not on your team;
Can't even make it,
Don't have to be old yet they're outdated,
Undeserving of the attention they receive.
Cause they never will
Due to the skills they lack,
Do not succumb to their pressure;
You are here to win, and you will
 Do not empower your heckler.

STAND

You are a life.
You were given a chance,
To be fruitful and multiply,
To stand.
Stand - you're supposed to,
Stand -it is in your nature
To stand -you were created to
Stand: you were given legs from your creator.
You will stand for something,
Whether you know it...or not;
So make your standing mean something,
And give what you stand for all you've got.
Cause you are neither here nor there for long,
The second you claim now has gone,
And the minute you've used cannot be
replaced
So there is truly not enough time in a day.
Standing implies one is willing to show they
are present,
But being present doesn't mean you are here;
So be here, when you stand, and leave your
presence:
 Let us know, when you stand, you have truly
appeared.

CANVAS

Blank.
We begin with a blank canvas.
Not knowing exactly where to begin,
Sigh...
We find the courage...and it begins.
Understanding this belongs to us;
Knowing this is brand new;
We use different tools, whichever one is
desired;
All in order for us to do what we came to do.
This is art;
Yours and Mine;
With every stroke of lead coming from
within;
And each brushing of the paint coming from
inside:
We compromise;
I mean we come together;
Creating a masterpiece:
You and I.
We have learned from what we have been
through,

We are prudent enough to know how to adjust,
And enjoy
To do that which we do not have to be sorry for:
Our Work,
Our Art,
Our US.

THE PEN

If I could place my heart in a pen: I would;
And I would have my heart write down
every word that it should;
My heart would scribble every single syllable
if it could,
Give written evidence of how I feel for you is
what it would do,
That's if I could:
Place my heart in a pen.

If my body could bungee into a Bic: I'd go;
And my body would begin to be descriptive
about descriptions
      that you have never read before;
The body would write unrestricted, the mind
would no longer control;
And you would know everything the body
wanted to do
      that the mind wouldn't allow before,
Before it happened is what I am referring to:
And my body was within an ink pen.

The last part of me I would ever want within
a pen would be my mind;
Because it might write you the truth when I
wish I was lying;
My wishes, and entire thought process would
be revealed to you....
    ..line by line...
And you would know exactly how what came
to be materialized;
So if it came down to it, my mind is where it
would end,
I'll express my mind best I can:
But I will never allow it inside a pen.

GREAT WOMAN

A great woman is wonderful,
A great woman has values,
A great woman is believable:
But she is unbelievable too.
She is outstanding and understanding,
She is bad but she's good,
Compassionate, with prominence,
Yet overtly stands out only when she should.
A great woman is inspiring,
She causes growth through her conversation,
Her maternal intangibles develop fruits in
my life:
She fertilizes my imagination.
You are an enriching factor,
A subtle fifth element,
Your essence is pure in substance:
H-E-A-V-E-N sent.

STRIVE

You take me for who you thought I was,
Rather than for who I am today.
From second hand information you choose to
judge;
A man who's character's shortcomings you
never witnessed on any day.
Like yard grass: we grow,
Yet for appearance's sake we require a trim;
So the grass you see on this present date,
Cannot be the same grass from back then.
That grass is gone, no longer with us,
What is present is what you see.
So when we've grown, our shortcomings are
cut,
And who we are is who we've grown to be.
In total fairness, Un-Arrest my development,
I live in a progressive state of mind.
Take me for who I am to you, in all
consciousness,
My best you'll find – in pursuit of my best is
how I strive.

WOMAN HOOD

An outlaw in her own right,
With a penchant for robbery;
A highly skilled archer with keen eyesight,
She could boast "Cupid ain't got nothing on
me."
She's a living legend,
A woman in the purest sense,
Winning the men, again and again,
She's notorious because of this.
She's noteworthy, with charisma,
Blameworthy for how she wins ya,
Guilty when she gets ya,
Yet you love her cause its in ya;
And she brings it out,
For that she's on the run,
She's a thief, a bandit,
But worthy of love so you give her some.

RESPOND

Respond...
Every time.
You must reply, so reply:
Right...as in the right way, the first time.
Do it;
Whether verbally or through action,
Please your Lord in how you respond:
And do it - when you know;
Act and live up,
Respond and promote our best,
Stay down for what is really up.
Learn and grow,
Apply and teach,
Reply when its your time to respond,
Each time it is you who the test may reach.

TAKE THE CAKE

You take the cake...
I wonder if you realize it;
Cause even though you know it took time for
me to be made,
You vaguely knew about it.
In your total disregard of how long it took to
prep me,
You came along being wonderful and fun,
yet, humble,
Then you made me disappear from the rest of
the party;
And through your personality I have found I
enjoy you,
Hope you don't give me away to anybody.
        Thank You for Taking The Cake.

SMOKING

Picking it up like it can't happen to you;
You tried it,
Hit it,
Now you have a habit,
And the habit is a part of you.
Known to cause cancer in California:
(The way the label warns ya);
Her effects are in you,
Her smell upon ya.
You see the signs,
Yet act as if you're blind,
And pick up, then light up:
One more time.
Hooked...
On the tip of your lips,
Giving you her butt to kiss,
You seek her and hunt her down,
 To light her again,
Desire has you gripped:
Can't live without taking a whiff.
She's Smoking.

THE IMPOSTER

Looks like,
Sounds like,
Meaning he speaks like you;
Acting like he,
As in pretending as if he,
Really wants what's best for you.

She is a test;
A trial,
Adverse to what you seek;
Contesting, competing,
As in conflict with,
Your newly found ability you have not seen.

The imposter,
Mr. Random Insinuation – Miss Spontaneous
Whisper,
The deliverer bringing doubt into your
mind's window;
Sabotaging your finish, having witnessed
your start,
The imposter infects your heart,
Using clever innuendo.

Arresting your greater self,
Kidnapping your best,
Keeping you from who you can grow to be.
The imposter is envious,
The imposter is jealous,
Arousing emotions which are not healthy.

Your best is in there,
You deserve to meet it,
You were created for excellence.
The imposter will hold you back,
And shut you down,
Preventing your understanding what your
lesson truly meant.

Shut down your imposter,
Be optimistic,
You can be prudent and not weak.
Find courage when you need it,
Bounce back when defeated,
In spite of the words the imposter may speak.

WHEN I CAN'T SPEAK

I see you and I want to speak.
I wish to speak words when it's you I witness.
My wardrobe of words becomes filled with
bodies,
Alive now, my chatter's chambers fill with
ammunition.
Phrases fight to be in the forefront,
Conjunctions prepared to bring about a
steady flow,
On standby to relay the message from within,
Ready to paint the portrait words want you
to know.
A dream would make this easier,
Then, my inexplicable limitations I could
readily accept.
Maybe then the explanation would become
much clearer,
As to why, around you, I breathe yet lose my
breath.
A voice-box with many priors;
A firing tongue ready to let loose;

Yet around you the voice-box follows the rules,
The firing tongue will not shoot.
The words which were alive become ghosts,
The loaded rounds transform into blanks,
I literally can't when I want to let you know,
Exactly what it is that I just cannot say.

MEMORY

As I sit alone I remember you,
It's like thoughts of you are uploaded into my
mind.
Clearly there on my mind's screen is you,
The woman whom I adore...right on time.
She always comes back and I always bring
her back;
Glad I can cause of how she moves me;
As if I touch her icon like an app,
And all of what she does comes alive in my
memory.
She is wonderful and makes me feel
stupendous,
She is an individual so there has never been a
her before.
A great woman and my mind: she's in it,
Wanting an S/D card to download her some
more.
I am telling the story of what this woman
does to me...
But she is awesome...
You probably would not believe,
So I will appreciate my time alone with my
favorite lady:
In my memory.

HE

It doesn't matter if you think I can.
He does.
He matters.
He imitates me perfectly,
But, he also cries if I cry.
He mocks me when I make faces that are
funny,
Yet, he's always honest –
He does not lie.
It doesn't matter if you think I cannot.
The man,
He believes;
Faithful for as long as I am;
Every time I believe I can face him,
He returns my stare;
He respects that I can, too.
As long as the man in the mirror believes in
me,
Your negative words do not matter:
I don't need you.

LIMITATION EVALUATION

What are limitations?
Are they self-inflicted, or voluntary
infections?
Are limitations temporary?
Is it morally based?
How long do limitations last?
Are limitations a state of being?
Do we have eyes, ears and a mouth?
Is there a brain in there?
What is a brain?
Are limitations trained to control our brain?
How did they come into existence?
Why were limitations invented?
Do mute people communicate?
What are these: signs?
Is there really a such thing as a limitation?

THE MODEL

Look at you,
You are beautiful.
Magnificent.
You are wonderful.
The components were taken:
We needed sugar, spice and everything
exceptional;
We needed sensuality, personality and a
beautiful smile too;
Wanted hair and needed wit,
A sense of humor, a presence authentic,
A belief in God as well, then we take in all the
measurements,
And The MODEL created was You: Excellent.

BY AND BESIDE

Missing you is like having you absent,
Having you absent, wanting you present is
what missing you is like;
It is your being there, yet you're not here;
Having you there and not with me is what
missing you is like.
Missing you is like a loss;
It is a loss because I gained when you came,
Came as in arrived and if you're not here
you're missing;
And if you are missing the present does not
amount to the same.
I miss you.
I want to be near you.
I wish I could hear you.
I want to be by you, like beside you, I miss
you.
Missing you is like leaving out something,
Something left out which is a necessary
ingredient.
It is like matter that doesn't truly amount to
nothing:
A sugar-free cake with nobody eating it.

Missing you is like crying,
Crying when there should be harmony;
But harmony can't be if I'm wailing,
Upset since I want you with me.
I'm strong but I miss you,
I have strength but you give me power,
I miss you yet I should have you;
My present should be our's.
I miss you.
I want to be near you.
I wish I could hear you.
I want to be by you,
like beside you,
I miss you.

VALUE IN WAITING

Since you have not arrived,
I am given opportunity to hope you will,
Then cause my smile – with your contagious
smile-
And a presence which is progressively better,
and better still.
You're not here but I look forward to when
you come,
It's like I'm forecasting a good woman's
arrival:
I see warm feelings and sunny skies, she's
second to none;
With no chance of thunderstorms or showers.
Whenever you get here I expect brushes with
greatness,
At the very least I imagine:
You'll arrive with an effortless gracefulness,
And speak as if nothing divine has just
happened.

Your absence is good while your presence
is anticipated;
You're so good I find I've found value in
waiting.

HANDICAP MATCH

Maybe the reason is these feelings I have;
Feelings which have me to see us up and on
top,
Not on our back;
I know we have ability – but are we the long-
shot?
Who is it that places a handicap in our
match?
What factors cause our advantage to shift?
Are there burdens, there, upon our backs?
Can it be our capabilities are dishonorable
gifts?
I do not see what they see,
I cannot see what you see entirely.
A wounded duck is not who I see in you, or
me.
In the mirror, a disadvantaged loser does not
look back at me.
What I have been through has given me
resolve;
It's as if I have become a champion through
rigorous training.

Even though I know I can never have it all,
In the face of our challenges, I still see us
gaining.
Winning begins within;
Please look in there and appreciate what
you've got.
Know you will win.
Believe you are a champion and not a long-
shot.

CULPRIT: COUNTERFEIT

What kind of love can you have;
If you cannot forget what you had;
If you continuously grab hold to what has
passed;
With what Was being to what you hold fast?
Are you a victim?
Again, when it is not happening today?
Are you still wounded when you should not
be injured?
And that love that hurt you has gone away?
Does love stand as the culprit?
Is it love who got you and still gets you?
Or was the perpetrator perpetrating;
And it was a counterfeit love who met you?
Dressing like,
Talking like,
Pretending to be a love they could never be.
It was not in their nature,
For them to epitomize love's nature,
And you found the lip-synching singer could
not sing.

Consider yourself blessed,
You saw through the fog,
You realized you were witnessing an act.
Love will come,
And be right when it does,
So be ready to give love back.

GET THE PICTURE

A picture of you is what's up to me;
It's just you, and I like who I see.
You're artistic in your poses,
And I doubt you even try to be,
But even if they say you are trying,
It sure looks like you are doing the hell out of
it to me.
Your smile is wonderful, your eyes are
beautiful,
Your lips are great, overall you're a handful.
I mean you're more than what they are,
You're like a newly invented card,
Nobody saw you coming,
But once played, we know you've won…by
far(hands-down).
If you're in the picture,
We want to know what's up wit cha.
You're the light, in the right spot,
With the right bottom, and right top,
With a nice cool, and the right hot,
If you're there we know who's fire makes
them not.

If a word were you:
People would slow down when they hear you,
Hoping whomever spoke you will repeat you;
If reading, they'd grab a dictionary after
they see you,
Wanting to know what makes you,
Why does it feel like this when we say you?
A song? We'd call the station to request you.
Get it from me: there's nothing like you.

FEE FOR YOU

If there was a fee I had to pay for you,
I would have to pay the fee for you,
Cause if there was a price for you,
Never could I allow anyone else to buy you.
If goons kidnapped you,
And called me on the phone:
I will do whatever it is they ask me to,
They will receive their ransom for you to
come home.
If the man was saying 75-85-95,
And you were being auctioned;
I would lift my paddle or wink an eye,
I would be the one who bought you.
If I walked by a store, on an unassuming day,
And saw you: Doll, in a window,
I would double-back and enter the store,
To get you out of that window.
I would say "I love that Doll! She's beautiful,
"She must be mine," you know.
They'd say "Okay, you know she's priceless?"
And slide me the fee on a note.
What I mean is the fee could never be too big,

For if you are still alive, I know you still live;
And if I know you're alive, I want you with
me,
No matter what Doll,
You're priceless,
I will have to hand over the fee.

IN MOTION

What is it that moves me,
When I move for love,
And love is either tardy,
Or consistently an absentee?
Could H_2O be what love's sum would be?
One H being my baby,
The other H being me,
With a breath of O to make our compound
complete?
Is a shower in love's moisture the thing for
which I dream?
Would I know, or,
Will I identify,
Or must rain reach our love as a seed?
What moves me when it is love I move for,
Is there optimism in my battery?
Can there be hope in the air blowing belief
when in motion,
Or am I healed from past hurts when burning
my gasoline?

Will love's promise ever be made to me,
Am I inadequate,
Would love speak to me, or am I imagining,
And love is mute, incapable of saying a
thing?
But how, when, where and what is it that
makes me do?
I'm still discovering,
And stop I cannot,
I must continue to move.

WANT

I want it more than you know,
I want it more than you can ever see.
I want it more than you choose to believe.
I want it worse than you.

My potential to grow exceeds any seed.
I will grow more than any seed can.
I said I want it.
My want eclipses hunger.
I'll have it - it'll be good -
One way or another, or six-feet under.

U.S.A.

If the world of women was America,
You would be America's Hawaii.
You are a state of womanhood,
Desired to be visited by many,
Standing alone from the mainland,
With your own identity.

UNANSWERED RHETORIC

If you could bring it all back to me,
What would I receive?
Would there be anything left for me?
What exactly would it be?
Jelly spread too thin is what your sweet is
like to me;
I am not overwhelmed,
I am disappointed,
On my toast you are unsatisfactory.
So what would I have if you did return?
Could there be anything added to myself?
Or are you a negative wishing to caboose my
equation,
Taking away from what I do have left?
How can I want what is no good for me?
Why do I desire a relationship which is
unhealthy?

INVESTED

Then you do not respond...
Or, you take your time...
You pray;
You know tomorrow is not promised;
Why live like it is?
With everything you do:
All the time you share...
Things you lend...
How much does it cost you?
Do you make sound investments?

TO: FOR

This is for the light you inspire;
For the ballet we attend every time you float
by;
Dedicated to the cool you epitomize;
Appreciative,
We Are,
For who you Are,
To: You
For: You
You are why we shine.

This is for the distinct, smooth sound of your
voice;
For the way you ask but leave us without
choice;
Devoted we become to do your will,
Enchanted - not ill,
Thankful to discover how magic feels,
For: You
To: You
In The Lord's Way, but in pursuit of you is
the direction we live.

This is for the twinkle in your eyes;
For the twinkle inside which storms my
insides;
Disperses a shock down my spine, every time,
Earthquakes shake my spirit,
And I want good for you,
For the good you make me feel,
To: You
For: You
You must be the best woman alive.

RAIN

Could there be,
Or would there be,
Had The Lord never created and allowed
there to be:
Rain?
Would that mean (from the way things are)
Another factor would have to change?
How self-sufficient are we?

WEIRD

He lives;
Yet, is a victim of conformity.
He gives from his heart,
"He's up to something," assumes the majority.
People attempt fruitlessly to catch his
number;
They call him weird, or some non-uniform
adjective or another.

In the mirror…
When staring, he loves who stares.
His love expands outside the mirror to
humanity;
Humanity expects him to be one of theirs.

He is comfortable within his skin;
Being any or everyone is absent from what
he intends.
He is genius.
He is independent, He knows who he is.
He is morally conscious in his ambitions.
But them he isn't, them labels him: Weird.

LOOPHOLE?

I bought a bracelet.
I stole a ring.
I paid for a necklace,
I get everything.
Look at my ride.
Look at my shoes.
Look at the shoes on my ride;
Look at how they shine dude.
Dressed to impress;
Dressed in the finest threads;
I do whatever it takes for the best;
Dressed and draped till I'm dead.
    Materialism religion like law;
    I got it all for real: Am I flaw?

MOCKERY

Half-heartedly;
As in not whole-heartedly;
Giving effort partially:
Mockery.
Limiting the possibility;
Preventing what could be,
By not doing anything,
When one knows how it should be:
Happening.
Being asked to go the distance,
Then one agrees to go the distance,
Yet behind your back they go half the
distance.
Speaking it yet never intending to go the
distance.
Not whole-heartedly.
As in giving effort partially;
Half-heartedly:
Mockery.

REINFORCEMENTS

It is inevitable: tough times will arrive.
In those times, the suggestion: call on these
guys.
"Guys" – One may refer to them as –
Reinforcements rendering assistance,
                              Aiding tough
times to pass.
Support your mind with positive substance;
                        Spoken or Written.
Substances you may send into a situation
          When you need adequate instructions.
Without entertaining them,
                        One may turn off a
rough road,
And detour onto a rougher one.
                  Find them
- reinforcements are everywhere –
                        Remember them
Their nature is to assist when tough times
come.
Entertainment of these mental beings makes
adjustment easier,

Artillery, subconsciously present, when
warring situations happen to occur.
We, as people, are inspired...Fearless: when
we have an army behind us.
We must recruit our reinforcements,
                    Overcoming is a necessity,
Our reinforcements will inspire and remind
us.

Arm Yourself
Your spirit will be served when you need
them,
Have Faith
- and when you see tough times -
They will not look so tough when you see
them.

FORGET YOU

Forget You.
Forget you is my current attitude.
Forget you because I imagined great times
with you.
Depart from my mind – you don't care about
me.

Grant me Solitude
Grant me solitude minus you.
Grant solitude to me, since, in terms of caring
for me...
You don't know how to.
Leave me alone. Solo is the best way for me to
be lonely.

Maybe you Can.
Maybe you can be a real friend.
Maybe you can give true friendship to me,
Or, do you give it all to them?
Are you spread too thin?
Take our optimism with you.
Allow me to stop imagining our possibilities.

Forget You.
Forget you is still my attitude.
Forget you in the name of advantages taken
by you.
Disappear from my mind, I'll get over you.
You only give a second thought about me in
my mind.
Forget You.

PLEASURE IN NEVER

Never in my life have I loved in eight days,
Never ever vowed forever in Ten,
Never said I never would so I guess I was
open to it,
And if I could I would do it all over again.
She's stirred emotions within me into
solutions never mixed
      Before:
             Her vibe is music,
                       And I'm still
dancing...
I've never moved to a tune like this before.
She infects my entire being,
With her perfect imperfections;
Makes me believe I can sing, or achieve
anything,
She's my prototype of a woman's
construction: perfected.

Never in my life have,
         And now that I have her I never
will again.
Now I've discovered my companion towards
forever,
I've achieved Never (with Pleasure) as long
as we are together
                              Till the end.

WHERE YOU BELONG

If I can, I will lead you by the hand.
If you will allow it, I will take you with me.
Our singles become a couple as we advance,
En route to where we're supposed to be.
When you're in my eyes: its magical when
you're there.
I appreciate you in my vision.
I can stand to always have you alive in there.
Doing my job: I'd make you my living.
I believe you belong with me.
The facts point towards you and I.
I adore you and our existence depends upon
you and me.
Simply because a man and woman's union
causes the population to rise.
We should go together and come together;
Reside together and abide as we can stand it.
You feel so good I pray that we Be: together,
Pledging our allegiance in the way Our Lord
planned it.

(UNTITLED)

Fluid...
Conforming to the shape of it's vessel,
 Filling it with all it has...
To give,
If it can,
If there is enough.
Meaning if it has the ability,
Can be half-full or half-empty.
Yet, it is there,
As much as it can be:
"It"
If it really "is"
"Love".

IMPRINTED

Touch Me.
Will you put your hands on me?
Can you reach out and grab me when you
touch me?
Will you leave your individuality upon my
being?
Do me right now that you have a hold on me.
Let me have pleasing encounters impressed
upon my memory.
Touch me in ways I will be pleased, please.
Do me how you want to be remembered by
me.
Our fingerprints are a show of our
individuality.
Our fingerprints are not identical to any.
We must understand this miracle collectively.
I know there is none other like you who can
touch me.
All I want is for us to be pleased when we're
done;

Well aware of what we do today which will
be left behind.
So when you touch, touch me with a touch
unmatched by anyone,
Leave me with prints of your identity, leave
me with your one of a kind.

TWO OF YOU

I fell asleep with you on my mind.
While I slept I dreamt of you.
In the dream there were two of you,
I was overwhelmed by the two.
When I realized I had met a beautiful
woman,
And I valued who she was:
I was confronted by an identical woman,
Who was everything she was.
Number Two - you too.
She had your charisma and your eyes,
Another who now was only like the other,
Her all was completely you.
It was astonishing and I was astounded.
A grandiose experience, I needed to remain
grounded;
So I remained true to myself, loyal to who I
met,
And walked away from who I didn't know
yet.

WITHIN

If you will, I want to;
If we can, I don't want to ever stop;
Not until we've done all we've come to do,
And we have surpassed our collective
proverbial top.
One always finds they can do more than
what they saw;
A person's vision limits what can realistically
be;
A realistic achiever finds themselves doing
more than they saw;
Since what actually happens we can't truly
foresee.
Our will to achieve seasons our
demonstration,
Our abilities are enhanced by our desire to
win;
So our capabilities are powered by our spirit,
Our ultimate victory comes from within.

LOST AND FOUND

After leaving,
The intensity of my heart-rate didn't
decrease,
Normalcy didn't return to my breathing,
And you were still there in every part of my
thinking.
I was gone yet not gone away,
My mind was trying to make sense of what
happened,
Bewildered about what transpired today,
When my body went away and my mind
remained.
I mean to say: physically I left – mentally I
stayed,
Physically I wasn't right since I left my
brain.
My mind there with you and the awesome
you portray,
My body over here in an awestruck state.

I mean today was brand new because I've never been here,
Never here to experience, it was like I found a buck,
And you were all the more amazing when I returned there,
Pleased when I arrived to pick my mind back up.
There you were, standing, all of who I wanted,
The live image of who was in my brain,
Yet and still a calmness overcame me at that moment,
When I had you within my eyesight and I could see you again.
You are an amazing woman,
One of a kind, there aren't any like you around.
You are the beauty behind me losing my mind with you,
Then having to return to recover it from lost and found.

LOVE THERAPY

Love has a way of searching for you;
A way of locating the lost one;
Bringing them to be absorbed;
To be absorbed and in love:
Again.
Love has a way of finding you;
A way of returning one who is far away;
Giving them resuscitation;
Causing them to be awakened;
Awakened by and alive with love:
All over again.
Love has a way of causing you to feel;
A way of curing paralysis,
One moves again,
Determined to stand;
Stand by and walk in love:
One more time.
Love has a way of showing you;
A way of proving it's everlasting quality;
Giving one loving qualities;
Causing them to have love's character;
Characteristics fueled by love,
Which will not compromise.

ALL OF IT

While I'm away from you,
I think of you,
It is like I'm never away from you,
During the moments in which I am
away...from you
I keep you in mind,
I believe I understand what we want,
I know our relationship isn't just mine,
So I don't do things which conflict with what
we want.
You're winning my heart,
I hope you want to win with me,
Cause if you win my heart you get all of me,
And I promise to show you what all of that
means.
So while you're not here,
Know that I keep you here,
You move me, you're in my spirit:
So you're never away,
You're always near,
Hope you recognize all of it when you get it.

COPILOT

You're my companion, and copilot,
You're my mate.
You're with me when I need understanding;
You always manage to make my day.
If and when I choose to stand:
You stand beside me, proudly, and hold my
hand.
When I decide things flyer than what normal
mammals usually do,
You get fly with me and come fly too.
When the time arrives and I need you there:
You show in my time of need, showing you
care.
You do you all the time every day,
My companion, my copilot, you're my mate.

I chose you over all that has been in the past,
I choose you in the present and as our future
lasts,
I offer my companionship to you in return;

And I'll fly with you as long as you'll learn;
Learn from me and I from you,
As we strive to fulfill our duties and all we
must do.
I offer you my attention and conversation,
I'll give my affection and we'll enjoy
recreation.
I offer you my everything, all I can get;
You're my mate, companion, my copilot.

SO-SUPERHERO

You make me feel right, you make me smile.
I like what our vibe feels like, and I haven't
liked in a while.
Your skin-tone, your smile... I hope I'm not
dreaming.
I like the way it feels, so don't pinch me (if I
am dreaming).
I'm an independent thinker,
*   And, I think you're wonderful.*
I think you're hot, I think you're cool,
I think make me feel phenomenal.
However long it takes does not matter to me,
The fact I know you're alive is intense – it's
inspiring;
I want to prove, I want to show you I can do
everything.
I want to be a factor in both our lives, I want
us to grow into being.
You are fuel on my masculinity,
A worthy release for my sensitivity,
I think you're fire woman (like I told you
before);
I like who you are – I like what I see.

You make me desire to be the man I am
supposed to be,
And I want good for you due to how good
your presence is to me,
You make me feel so-superhero…

                             You charge me.

You make me feel right woman, you make me
smile;
Your eye-contact , your vibe, I like how you
smile.
I like how you B-E, I like how you stand;
I like how you inspire M-E, you inspire the
superhero in a mortal man.

IN YOUR EYES

There is life within your eyes,
I see it when your eyes are within mine,
I close my eyes and remember you in my
mind,
And I feel how it feels, intensely...in my
insides.
I care less about what they think,
I am all the more concerned with who you
are.
Sideline stalkers have no place in our league,
All they can do is watch us from afar;
Cause our attraction causes my equation to
gain exponents I appreciate;
I mean you square me like the second power,
You charge through the way we
communicate,
And I hope our mutual mine becomes ours.
Cause you are the lady that motivates,
I told you before you're the reason behind the
superhero.
It takes you and I for life to perpetuate,

So what's a greater reason to have me save the world for?
Lady you're the oasis which sits deep in my life's desert,
You're the refreshment after extreme conditions I've survived.
You're the figment that I wish to understand fully,
And I imagine I will when I look in your eyes.

STAR

When you're in the mirror, recognize the star
looking at you.
Know who she is and remember what she's
been through.
Keep in mind she was born to win in
whatever she may do;
Created with the capacity for excellence: it's
in you.
You are the main attraction.
In your life you are the lead.
Our Lord being The Director of the action:
Your life's movie will be judged by your
deeds.
You are an awesome personality.
You are soothing, epitomizing maternity.
A mother, A woman, you are a lady;
You are the star in the mirror who we're
blessed to see.
     The star in the mirror is who you should
know,
     You are the star, its clear in how you
play your role.

EXPRESSIVE

Expressive, suggestive,
Remarkable, Unique;
Inspirational, sensational:
Compelling me to speak.
She.
She is...
She is Her,
All of her is who I see.
Comforting, soothing,
The woman for whom I dream.
Created for excellence, she enhances my
abilities;
With the addition she is,
By the way of the woman she is:
Her - "her" enhances me,
Through her expressive presence,
With her suggestive aura which gracefully
interrupts my individuality,
I am drawn to her as in stuck to her earth
like gravity.
For the sensation;
For the inspiration of my expression;
For her all;
For: Her.

ENHANCEMENTS

It's you baby;
This realization has me smiling;
Cause I've been even better lately:
Since your showing where you are, as if you
were hiding.
Shadowed in darkness,
Concealed in my life's night;
Sunshine has shown herself in my life,
And I see my bests arrive before my eyes,
It's you sweetheart.
A beautiful, genuine, inspiring, specimen;
A real woman, and from here you stand out
and apart,
You're a masterpiece, a living, moving, work
of art.
It's all you;
And this is for all that you do.
For the efforts you give behind the scenes to
make things come to,
To all that we witness: this is in appreciation
of you.

Cause at first I didn't know,
But then it began to show,
Your addition has helped me to go,
And your you has enhanced My "who I was"
before.

ALWAYS

Remember who you are;
Don't forget where you have been;
Be served well by those events which didn't
tear you apart;
Be exceptional: again and again.
You are here to BE;
BE... Live Up.
You'll find it requires equal energy,
If you insist upon the same stuff.
Know that you can,
Remember God and be diligent in your days;
He never forgets you, His work is forever
working;
Everlasting: Always.

GOOD

Created.
You, Me...Them: Everyone.
Given life from the same source;
With provisions available for everyone.
The creation.
The earth:
Functions perfectly and abides;
Abides by the law of its origin;
The Originator;
For Good;
Until its perverted or misunderstood.
From the source of good,
To bring about your greater self:
From within.
To have you remember Him.
He never forgets you:
Your creator:
The origin of good.

PRIDE

Pride.
The root of evil.
Being better than,
Making one worse than,
And opposed to:
You.

Pride.
A feeling.
What one feels when they're spending,
After one has what they're getting;
And they see the reaction from:
You.

Pride.
An adverb.
Describing.
Could make things right if channeled
correctly,
And not used disrespectfully:
Should be understood and not misused.

PAINFUL LOVE

Thoughts of her assault my memory,
Regularly.
Renewing the injury;
The injuries.
Why did she?
How could she?
Hurt me, disappoint me,
She was a hero to me;
She didn't know how to love me.
There were always discrepancies.
Things...
Too much for me...
Things...
Too much for me to believe.
Things...
Which affected me.
I loved her unconditionally.
But she couldn't,
And when she tried it was too late.
How can I? How could she?
How can love do this to me?

KEEP IT MOVING

I look and keep it moving;
I have to;
Even though the sound of your voice is so
soothing,
Now, I know, isn't the time for me to be near
you.
I see you with me,
My vision picture perfect...I smile,
I'm aware I'm only imagining,
With today incapable of possessing our
portrait's time.
I witness you when you pass,
And I know you're not passing by to remain
for long,
Its rejuvenating...
        Better yet: I feel right,
           I value those moments,
      Even though they do not last long.
They do and they don't;
        An impact that doesn't disfigure;
I hope you will stay, yet I know you cannot,

My heart speaks:
I want be with you.
I have to look and keep it moving;
Our day has not yet arrived;
I hear you say "Hello" as we're commuting,
 And I return your greeting with a smile.

ON MY BACK

With my back on the mattress,
My head on the pillow,
My eyes towards the attic,
My mind out the window...
I think of You.

With my back against the mattress,
My thoughts drift...I'm lonely.
My body a soliloquy, without speech;
Its saying my mate should be here,
Of companionship: I'm deserving...
Without a single sound here that you hear.

With my head disfiguring the pillow,
My eyes towards the attic,
My mind out of this atmosphere:
I dream you will not let me go,
If you ever decide to have me,
Our bond being the break point,
And I begin to win from here.

With my back on the mattress,
My head against the pillow,
My eyes attempting to envision what can be.
My mind is on you,
Even though it cannot touch,
Filled with optimism, great intentions and
sincerity.

.

MS. ONE OF A KIND

Ms. One Of A Kind this is for you.
The woman persistently on my mind is who
I'm writing this to.
This is for you Ma'am and all that you do.
One Of A Kind Woman this, I say again, is
for you.
While trying to find my way I found you.
There is no way for me to have already knew
you would be like you.
I found a priceless treasure wrapped in the
same skin which wraps you;
A beautiful Doll who smiles just like you do.
In the essence of our creation I was created
for you.
There could never be any one without two;
Except as our Lord will's cause He is who
gave me a chance with you,
And put our compatible pieces near, allowing
us to do what we do.
It was here when our spirits found one
another,

Each conscious of what it wanted, calling out
to the other.
Calling out with the intent to discover:
The missing pieces possessed by the other.
We made it here and I get teary-eyed,
I look forward to the day when we get there,
Get there like be there as in when we arrive,
I want to be there with you Ms. One Of A
Kind.

MAGIC

Captivated...
Drawn In...
Looking...
Anticipating,
Observing:
The chronological order.

As the stages unfold,
From step one to two:
Three if necessary,
And then is when;
There is where.....
You have me yearning for the moment.

The way you do;
The in between,
As I begin to imagine you cannot;
Then you do - and it gets me:
I smile - its warming.
Magic.

MIDAIR

I had to say good-bye;
It was time for me to fly
Within, my insides spoke why,
For now: it was just that time.
Leaving with I LOVE YOU rolling from my
tongue,
Hoping and having faith my feelings will be
felt,
And if they touchdown and score like One,
I'll know for sure you care.
What is it that happens when words travel?
Percussions from a person's physical?
Reeds, winds and acoustics roll and unravel,
The body, alone, working an instrumental.
Various sounds understood as speech;
Vibrations of sound-waves in air,
Giving you what I feel when I speak,
Traveling from here to there.
I left the Love Words that left me: airborne,
Unable to witness it land within you;
Knowing its expression from my end felt
warm,
Hoping that once you catch it you feel warm
too.

EVERY TIME I SEE YOU

When I see you...
I see a noun in a very grand sense:
A person, a place and a thing; you are all of
this.
I mean you're all of that,
All of the person who inspires me.
A place because being around you is an
event,
Around you is everywhere I want to be.
You are so *not* normal,
And your abnormalities make you a thing;
You're a beautiful woman so don't get it
twisted,
You just overshadow the qualities of normal
beings.
You are the exception,
You are excellent,
You were created for it.
You are the blessing,
You excel,
And we are captivated by the rate you are
going.

I mean you must be going or doing
something,
I believe
Because you're still alive.
And you get there, go there
And arrive without driving
Simply because a being like you flies.
If this is an illusion
Don't show me how you do it
Just continue to do how you do.
You touch me with your presence
And I love how it feels
Each and every time I see you.

DESIGNER GARMENT

Your jeans don't fit me,
Your shirt isn't my size,
Just because you wore it
Doesn't mean I should make it mine.
I am somebody.
I am one of a kind.
Your design isn't what makes my body;
My individuality is all mine.
What you've made doesn't make me fit in.
What you've worn doesn't give me access.
Their name, worn by you?
I don't see how that makes my best.
I am more than what I wear;
I am who's beneath the outfit.
I can take who I am anywhere;
Content of my character is the superior
garment.
Your jeans do not fit me,
Your shirt is not my size,
Maybe if you made your character better
fitting,
Then would be when I might make it mine.

NEW CLOTHES

Where it comes from I don't know,
And I can't understand where it goes,
The intensity;
The feeling:
When I know I have on nice clothes.
There is nothing new under the sun,
But I cannot deny what new clothes have
done,
To me -and for me,
It is a destination to which
                I wish
                To return from where I've come.
To that feeling there...
        Where...what I wear has me...
But am I already there...
        And can't I.D. my insecurity?

SATISFIED(incomplete)

Here I am with my pen in my hand,
Thinking of the lady who satisfies who I am.
Her presence does something to me.
She does something to me as in she moves me.
I do what's happening on her and my behalf;
I do it in appreciation of life and she has no
need to ask.
But if she asks of me then she shall receive;
Whatever it is that it may be, whatever it is
that she may need.
And if I have to go far for her then I will
travel,
I'll go the distance in order to compel our best
to unravel.
I'll do what I should since she inspires me to
be better;
I'll even write her poetry and author love
letters.
For her, cause she is: her; and there isn't
another like her who I've met.
She's one of a kind, she's on my mind and I
feel her in my chest.

*She's something like them simply because they
share similar characteristics;
But they're nothing like her cause she's not
them believe me: there is a difference.
I can only imagine what our future will truly
grow to be,
I'm a man of faith so our present days I'll
manage how we need...*

GROWN

I am the man you met;
The person whom you ran into;
The fellow who you grew to know,
The individual you became attracted to.
The man you met is who I am;
I'm the extended version of who you liked;
An elaboration of who you were attracted to
says I;
Here to be who you were brave enough to
give a try.
We have grown;
And seeds only grow from the likeness of
what is sown;
It is incumbent upon me to always be the
man you have known;
With enhancements cause you've aided me to
be better, it has shown;
You are the woman who I met;
The one who inspires my best;
The person who I ran into,
The lady who has me optimistic about what I
haven't seen yet.
The woman who I've met is who you are;

You are my ride in love like you are a car;
I pray for a road trip which ends at a
magical place;
We may require refueling, rest or a changed
tire but we shall overcome.
Representing for ourselves each and every
day.
We must be who we are here to be;
And to what we require we should submit;
With our intent being sound as we sow our
seeds;
Our garden will flourish because of it.

TALKING REFLECTION

I am reminded of my passed life in more
ways than one;
Reminded of the trials, the tribulations and
of course how they've come.
"Is it my fault?" I ask "That I am forced to
live this life?"
Then it hits me on the second time around,
sometimes it does take twice.
All of the tests I go through are more than
mere chance;
So I pick my head up, cause in the end it will
be I who will have chance to dance;
Dance, rejoice, celebrate and thank The Lord
above,
For blessing me with my third eye, now that's
true love.
"Foolish things you may feel will only get in
your way,
"On top of unorthodox actions you'll pay for
later, if not today,
"You are a unique individual, when will you
realize this and continue to grow?

"Go, I say: go, cause what lies ahead you will never know.
"The world will not stop it's rotation, so neither can you;
"So when the guy in the mirror says "Shawn you've made it!"
"You'll only smile because you already knew."

Appreciation

THANK YOU!
This collection was written from the heart.
I am grateful that you chose to take the time
out to check me out. I pray that my voice has
been a soothing one.

Find Me@:
www.shawnlavette.net

lavettepublishing@yahoo.com

www.ingramcontent.com/pod-product-compliance
Lightning Source LLC
Chambersburg PA
CBHW070527030426
42337CB00016B/2138